LOOK, NO HANDS!

LOOK, NO HANDS!

CLAIR KILLEN

*For David
with love
Clair*

MANY NAMES PRESS

1999

COPYRIGHT © 1999 CLAIR KILLEN
9595 STERLING CREEK ROAD
JACKSONVILLE, OR 97530

COVER ART AND TEXT FORMATTING © 1999
KATE HITT
PRINTED AND PUBLISHED IN THE US
AT MANY NAMES PRESS
POST OFFICE BOX 1038, CAPITOLA CA 95010
www.manynamespress.com

ISBN: 0-9652575-8-4
ALL RIGHTS RESERVED. FIRST EDITION.

Genevieve Windsor, Garrett Miller, Joan Peterson,
Doug McClellan, Toni Van Deusen,
Sara Jameson and Kate Hitt

I appreciate the ways each of you
opened doors for me.

Thank you

Table of Contents

Private Show 1
Words and Doors 2
Up Periscope 3
Long Before Joe Camel 4
My "Danse Russe" 5
Whenever 6
Flying Blind 7
Routine 8
Switchbacks 9
Encounter Group 10
The Edge 11
Bump, Bounce and Oh Boy! 12
Hands 13
It Was Worth It 14
A Winter Day 15
No Place to Hide 16
I Knew It Was Thursday 17
Big Man 18
Reunion 19
Seventeen 20
Birth of an Outsider 21
Hard Days 22
Different Folks 23
My Mother Fought Her Father 24
Loose and Empty 25
Sister 26
Rhonda 27
Priceless Gift 28
It's Time 29
Surprise Visit 30

Time To Let Go 31
Seven Year Ritual 32
Another Love Story 33
Short Fuse 34
This Saturday Afternoon 35
Questions 36
Alone 37
How It Is 38
A Gift Remembered 39
Home At Last 40
For the First Time 41
The Prize 42
First Snow Today 43
Here and Now 44
Always Questions 45
Saga 46
an Invitation 47
Old Photographs 48
The Finish Line 49
Age Like a Desert 50
Back and Forth 51
What About It 52
Observation 53
More Than Meets the Eye 54
Lightness of Being 55
Spring Cleaning 56
Old Soldier 57
I Want to Talk 58
What Then? 59

SUMMER WRITERS IN IOWA CITY 60
ODE TO A PROFESSOR 61
ALLIHIES 62
NEW MEXICO STORY 63
PROGRESS REPORT 64
AND TREES AND BEETLES KNOW 65
IT'S NOT THAT FAR FROM HERE 66
NOW SHOWING 67
REINCARNATION 68
NOT THE FIRST TIME 69
MIRROR 70
LAST DAY 1995 71
ON CHRISTMAS MORNING 72
A DAY ON TWENTY-THIRD STREET 73
NO CHANGE FOR THE BUS 76
WE JUST KEEP ROLLING ALONG 77
OASIS 78
LONG RED MANICURED NAILS 79
MEMORIES OF EMMA LOU 80
RICHARD FEYNMAN 81
GOODBYE TONY / AN INVITATION 82
JACK'S STORY 83
ENLIGHTENMENT NEXT STOP 84
WINNER TAKE ALL 85
EVENT 86
LOOK AWAY 87
ONE CAMERA ANGLE 88
WHAT IS IT GOING TO BE? 89
YEAR END 1998 90

Private Show

Writing poems and stories
like a strip-tease dancer,
the audience shouting

More! Take off more!

Hat away like a frisbee, shoes
kicked down the runway, shirt and pants
into the crowd, shorts for the first row.

"G" string and tassels drop away.
My heart watches, hesitant,
like a stripper's blank eyes.

Words and Doors

The wastebasket overflows
with yellow-lined fits and starts,
spent ammo that missed its target.

Some with one word, a line,
a stanza, some full sheets,
stillborn. Sometimes

an anxious chest guards
old records of being mugged
and confusion when being hugged.

Like buried plutonium
radiating demons with half-lives
longer than a lifetime.

Wait a minute! T h a t ' s w a y t o o l o n g !

Dare I tear off doors,
enter with whip and chair,
outlast growls, beady eyes,

make them shape up,
stand aside, allow live words
to break out and dance?

Up Periscope

Something about a feather lying in weeds
beside the dirt road on my land. Strange—
third one in a month, each unexpected
on a different day, not far apart.

Two white ones with black triangles
along the trailing edge, then one
yesterday, golden brown and white
except for the end, a dark brown square.

I gave the first two to a friend. She said,
"Listen! You are being sent a message."
This rattles my cage. I sail the fourth quarter
on dead reckoning, at my own pace.

These god-damn feathers could be a message
from the universe to my unlisted telephone.

Long Before Joe Camel

I smoked at fourteen. At fifteen had my first beer
and a pork pie hat. I lit stick matches with my thumb,
book matches with either hand. Lighters were for sissies.

At thirty-three, four packs a day, eyes red,
I coughed all the time. One day driving, my left hand
pulled a stick from my shirt pocket while

one burned in my mouth, another
burned in my right hand. I screamed,
       "Who's running my life? I quit! I quit!"

My body shook, head ready to explode, I didn't tell
anyone for a week, a madman with my family,
an asshole with my friends.

I missed those sticks a long time.

My "Danse Russe"
William Carlos Williams

I was eighteen, high on beer when
I read a poem by a poet who danced naked alone
late at night. I danced bare-ass to Artie Shaw.

He lived in New Jersey, wrote poems
for his neighbors, not in England prancing
with Elliot and Pound.

He delivered two-thousand babies
wrote as many poems, was never afraid
of danger from his words.

When the poet was seventy, I was thirty-three.
Separately our loyalty was questioned.
We both outlived Joe McCarthy.

Whenever

I always wanted a real sailboat. In my boyhood dream
she was white and fast, with a purple spinnaker
and never needed work.

At forty I bought one, fiberglass hull, teak top-sides
designed to race and cruise. I named her "Whenever"
in gold letters: *better whenever than never.*

On windy days I stole time, headed for white water.
At the tiller, soaked in cold spray, legs braced,
I looked up and screamed,

Stop me if you can, whoever you are!

Duty stopped me, her teak dried, turned gray,
a garden of barnacles covered her bottom,
sails molded, fittings corroded, her engine died.

I sold her cheap to a young man
with a strong body, lots of time to take her in his arms,
love her, and raise her sails again.

Flying Blind

He drove to town through mountains
in fifteen minutes, flat, down-shifting,
straightening every turn in the road.

He didn't remember much along the way,
the smear of oak, fir and pine as he flashed by,
maybe even the deer, dead or alive

purple lupine, golden poppies, iris
in bloom, horses, cows, and sheep in fields
covered with green grasses and alfalfa.

He didn't see any of it, not even ducks in ponds.
He was already in town, waiting for his car.

Routine

On liftoff over the Embarcadero
a jolt-crack sound, the chopper shook
shuddered, dropped like a stone.

I squeezed my daughter's hands.
        "Damn! They must be kidding."

A deep hard splash into the bay
just north of the bridge, fifty yards
off shore. Whimpers and screams
unrehearsed, out of control.

A desperate pilot kept bent rotor blades
turning to keep the tipped bird afloat,
while helpless freeway spectators,
news cameras watched.

When jurisdiction egos were satisfied
a Coast Guard cutter charged the blades
secured the bird, carried us to hard ground.

We were alone on the next flight to Oakland.

Switchbacks

With guides we rode over snow-covered Kearsarge Pass
to fish the Sierra for wild mountain trout. Twenty of us
out of Lone Pine with gear, food, and booze for forty men.

We caught goldens in raging Bubbs Creek and rainbows
in ice-shored lakes. After two days of too many men
and too many fish I headed up a steep trail alone.

On the trail a solitary backpacker
without guides, horses, mules,
or a ton of supplies.

"Jesus Christ!" I said.

The startled man welcomed me. He spoke
of hiking high country alone, showed his worn gear,
John Muir's book and maps.

The next year on top of Glenn Pass, alone,
I entered a new world of rock covered slopes,
alpine forests and high lakes.

For forty years the mountains kept me strong,
saved my body, gave me time to find switch-backs
for life in the flatlands.

Encounter Group

I was a tight outsider in a tense circle
of still strangers on pillows. Everyone with blank stares,
elevated heart-beats. My anger, a locked volcano

primed to explode. I pulled the leader down
to make him small. We crashed in the center
of the bulge-eyed group, rolled over and over,
        no rounds.

In fast sweat with pounding chests we collapsed,
the leader on top of me. When breath returned,
he rose, his arm cradled my head.

He looked into my streaming eyes and said,

        "You are stronger; I am younger.
        Are you ready to work?"

The Edge
(with thanks to Louis Simpson)

Two weeks over the Sierra, alone, off trails,
up and down steep slopes, beyond trash,

I crossed rampaging creeks, bathed and fished
canyon pools. Lightning stormed every day.

My last afternoon, impatient – I won't wait
for morning, I'll race daylight to my truck.

I drop down a deep chimney. A sheer cliff offers
the only way to clear a glacier, to roll over snow

then dance down four thousand feet over rocks
and boulders into a freezing lake.

I am cold-wet bruised, tired. It's dark
when a dirt road, then my truck appear. Home.

I am alone. I know where I've have been:
s e a r c h i n g   f o r   t h e   O x .

Bump, Bounce and Oh Boy

My socks soaked, down I sail
on a narrow Irish road on a bicycle.
Cars roar by just clearing
my right elbow.

I can't see bumps and pot holes.
Brakes wet, I can't slow down.
On my left side a smear
of uneven stone walls.

I am unsteady and frightened
moving so fast and excited!
On the next hill slowing, I shout,
   "Come on legs! Let's do it!"

They pump and my lungs
pump air and my bike
carries me up the long hill.
   "Body, I love you. We can go anywhere".

At the top, getting off tired–
my right leg catches the seat
and down we go bike on top of me
in a soggy ditch.

Under a gray sky, and a smell of grass,
an easy breeze, I am laughing.
Light rain blesses my face and neck,
my chest rocking the bike up and down.

Hands

Both hands trapped,
        deep cuts across my wrists,
        blood, hands almost lost.

Hands that took months to heal,
        new flesh, skin.
        I tremble every time I think,
            No hands!

Hands that pushed the floor to stand
        found pleasure within reach
        hid fists in pockets.

Hands that caressed curved surfaces
        entered warm moist places
        pulled softness close.

Hands that used micrometers, saws and hammers
        carried placards, slugged scabs
        sent messages with fingers.

Hands that touched so lightly
        wanted to reach out
        hesitant, held back.

Hands that waved goodbye
        wiped away tears

Hands that never prayed.

It Was Worth It

I tripped on the sidewalk edge,
crashed down in front of the library,
books, compact disks everywhere.
My knuckles, knees and elbows

slid on rough cement. People
stopped, asked if I was ok.
It's embarrassing to be old,
a giveaway of changing conditions.

I said I was fine, got up,
tried not to limp, laughed as I
visualized the lead-up events.

Out of my car I crossed the grass
and there before me two young
women walking with outstanding
breasts in tight sleeveless sweaters.

As they moved away, my eyes
followed two divine pairs
of round cheeks held
lovingly in tight blue jeans.

A Winter Day

Two weeks after two women were murdered
either for being gay or some reason,

the same day thirty-six cars crashed on ice
on Siskiyou summit. Three days after

the Bosnia cease-fire peace accord, the President
and the Republicans couldn't agree,

shut down government again.
Wind-chill was minus forty in Ames, Iowa.

No Place to Hide

He was asleep when I took his keys
to my dirt fort in the vacant lot down the street.
My mother's panicked voice yanked me home.

Red eyes angry, face unshaven,
my father pointed a finger, fired his cigarette breath,
    "The keys! Where are the keys?"

I couldn't look at them, didn't know
what to do but shake and say,
    "A big dog ate them."

He screamed words I can't remember,
slapped my ass and stormed away.
After we found the keys he was sorry.

It was the only time he ever hit me.

Knew It Was Thursday

when the smell of fresh bread baking
came from the brown frame house next door.

The family had six children, two dogs,
a cat, and a cage full of canaries.

Neighbor kids gathered like pigeons
for the mother's smile, and her cookies.
We competed to cut her grass.

The dad kept the house and car fixed, had time
to show us how to make kites and toys
with spools, string, sticks, and rubber bands.

My mother loved the sun, was an avid reader,
a vegetarian, barefoot most of the time.

My father was often away. I knew he would leave
when my mother's eyes faded. He would smoke more
              and go fishing alone.

Big Man

Blue eyes, blond eyelashes,
your breath hard, fingers brown,
a smoker who coughed incessantly,
spit frequently,
                and your breath —

You were thirty-nine years old.
After your shirts were washed
there was still the smell of you.

You were gone most of the time
chasing visions of a better world
for working people and their children.

I had your name but no way to connect —
You, always impatient, your message clear:

      Dream.
           Keep busy.
                Keep moving.

Always pay the bill.

REUNION

"Please come."
He never asked before.

I found him emaciated
in a county hospital ward
coughing spit into a paper cup,
forty-three, a chest full of tumors.

The gurney stopped in front of me.
He raised up on his bony elbows,
turned, and said quietly,

    "Take care of your mother and sister."

Before I could touch him or say a word
he dropped back on the pillow eyes closed
was wheeled away.

I never saw him again except in my dreams.

Fifty years later I was moving fast
down a steep mountain trail. On a switch-back
he came walking through my mind
blue eyes hesitant.

I held him tight, couldn't let go.

SEVENTEEN

I walked slow,
arms around my mother and grand mother,
sister under my right hand.

Outside the hospital
coal miner families, men, hats in hand,
women holding small bouquets of wild flowers.

"He's gone," I said.

He rescued those miners in 1935.
Kept them from starving after they lost
a long bloody Tennessee coal mine strike.

A hawk-faced preacher
named my Wobblie father a son of the Lord.
I ran home in crazy rage–
       smashed at birch logs with an axe.

Birth of an Outsider

We lived in neighborhoods with religious Jew-haters.
Their children warned of kikes.

Named and look Irish, inside angry,
ashamed of my fear.

When safe I said, "My father was Scotch-Irish,
my mother a Russian Jew. They were not religious."

Always the goy in front of the Jew.

I knew about lox, bagels, and borscht,
about Einstein, pogroms and Saturday services
for believers with yarmulkes.

I was a half-Jew with ten Yiddish words,
mixed pride and a connection to sadness,
the Torah, Hebrew, Yom Kippur, mysteries.

I wonder that I never married a Jewish woman
and something about the business
of never belonging anywhere.

Hard Days

My boys dropped from the nest, onto
hard ground. Their teacher wasn't there,
too busy, never had patience, nor made time.

I gave them things they could have worked for,
felt good about, strong. My dad wasn't there either.
In those days there wasn't any money.

At ten I delivered newspapers after school,
manned a corner weekends. My earnings made
a difference even when my dad worked.

When he worked he got paid on Saturday
came to my corner, bought all my papers,
stuffed them in a trash can and took me home.

Different Folks

Mine didn't honor holidays or leaders,
    renounced all religion,
        denied God, and the flag.

Fought for change,
    didn't hate anyone
        except fascists, capitalist pigs,
            and narrow-minded people.

My fourth grade teacher freaked
    when she heard me say there was no God,
        the principal sent me home.

I got the ten commandments without the cross
    from my folks, philosophers, and writers,
        Steinbeck, Sinclair, Veblen and Tolstoy.

I guess for me, everything is possible.
        It has to happen to me – to be real.

MY MOTHER FOUGHT HER FATHER

and the Rabbi in Russia, the system
in Philadelphia in garment sweat shops
alongside Emma Goldman.

She didn't believe in God, married a Wobblie,
a blond Irishman with blue eyes
who sang Joe Hill songs.

She wore see-through blouses in 1920,
smoked cigarettes through elegant holders,
said free love was fine.

She had hazel eyes, long curly black hair,
ate vegetables and fruit, garlic on black bread,
worshipped the sun.

A widow at forty-five, she never remarried,
wouldn't support herself, didn't age well,
slipped deeper in sadness.

Loose and Empty

We moved through traffic, siren quiet,
my one hand over her heart,
the other lightly touching her face,
my voice covering her with soft words.

Four beds in the hospital room,
an orange tree outside her window,
The doctor said, "She won't last."
I said, "Don't keep her alive."

Each day my mother grew smaller.
Her roommates didn't stay long—
each left on a gurney forever.

Each day the distance to her grew,
a fist in my chest, I couldn't stand it,
I wanted her gone.

I brought her a flowered bed jacket,
white lace blouse, a red ribbon for her hair.
The nurses helped her sparkle like a queen.

When I told her I would be gone a week,
"but I'll call every night," a shadow
moved across her face

The first night her voice slow, low.
The fifth, my wife said, "Come home."

A screen was around her bed. My body tight,
hers warm, loose, and empty.

SISTER

The second woman in my life,
    four years younger,
        a problem.

One time I pushed beads up her nose,
    another, grabbed her cat,
        swung it by the tail onto the roof.

I conspired against her with our mother.
    She forgave me, followed me around,
        wanted to be liked.

She was given dancing lessons,
    a boy's haircut,
        a way out.

She left,
    I stayed a long time.

When she came to visit
    I had tight feelings in my chest,
        almost couldn't breathe.

RHONDA

On a clear afternoon my
two-year old grand daughter
pulled her mom and dad down
a path covered with red maple leaves

to a neighbor's barn for
her first pony ride. When her father
forced the rusty gate, the wall
collapsed on Rhonda quicker

than they could scream.
After twenty-seven years
when small children play
we still look away.

Priceless Gift

My sister lived on New York's
lower east side south of Delancy Street
in a tiny flat over an old Orthodox synagogue.

A time of hope — remember Picasso's
peace dove? — she sculpted her version,
high-fired in brown clay. To hold it

eyes closed, a treasure. I couldn't let go.
She said it was her favorite piece
and gave it to me.

"How could you give me your favorite piece?"

She looked at me and laughed,
"I have twenty better ones I haven't done yet."

It's Time

There was my just-born daughter,
second row, smooth red hair,
so perfect. My throat was tight.

At night she doubled up,
cried. I held her against my chest,
walked slow, rocked her gently,
till her small body softened.

The words "I love you"
have always been bones in my throat.
She has never been as soft to hug
as those times I walked and rocked her.

It took me so long to crack an old door
slammed before she was born.

She just turned fifty.
Now I can tell her how
I love her.

Surprise Visit

He woke groggy in a room,
left eye bandaged, right blinded
by reflected sunlight, everything else dark.

He turned, felt stainless bars,
saw tubes in his shaved right arm,
his name on a plastic bracelet,
and high on the wall, a TV.

Light bounced off a glass covered
picture of a stream in a green
high mountain meadow. At the door
a gray drape on a ceiling track.

Next to the east window
he saw himself – old
in a soft blue easy chair.

Time to Let Go

Mountain ridges fence a canyon,
a squirrel flashes in a tree,
dog-shit on a gray shale road,
a flood of sunlight. He walks

under firs and pines, kicks
a rock and thinks about
simple issues that became
acts of betrayal.

The driver who cut him off,
a wait-person who served him
coffee in a cracked cup.

They didn't even know him.

Seven Year Ritual

Often at five pm at the Hide Out bar they met
in a corner booth, two drinks delivered quick.
Hands touching hands, moist thighs, eyes alive.

One car to the motel, usually number seven.

Five-thirty, explorations, deep breaths
and purring sounds. A half pint, Seven-up,
cigarettes stretching the moment to forever.

A seven year game, a quick glance and the plan,
routine polished, satisfaction guaranteed
as long as time was limited.

Sometimes more than an hour, more than a day.
After love-making not much to talk about,
not much to share.

Neither ever said, "I love you".

Another Love Story

Twenty years younger, blond, cocky, blue eyed,
street-wise, good looking, she was too young
for me, but, what the hell!

In a fencing match of words and stories, she said
she wanted a child but didn't want the father.
I said, " I wouldn't want you for a mother."

She drank her champagne and left. I finished my dinner alone,
found her walking in the shadows. My Porsche
her best offer for a no-words ride home.

Six-months later she was free again, current lover gone.
My offer accepted, dinner in Reno,
the late lounge show, breakfast in bed.

On a trip to New York, Tiffany's grabbed her,
every light turned on. "Can I have that sapphire bracelet?"
Outside the store, I raged in her face,
"How dare you! That cost a fortune!"

Her eyes narrowed, finger to my nose.
"You bastard! Don't trash my fantasies.
I have a right to ask. You have a right to say no!"

SHORT FUSE

We sat stiff at a small table, eyes on guard,
confrontation held at bay. Wine.
        A break in tension.

No matter who walked first, both
had been gone a long time. Possibilities
buried deep under sacred judgments.

Trivia cut an invisible line,
anger looked from side to side
to avoid being seen.

A chain of unfinished business,
one wouldn't talk, let it go, move on.
The other hurt, frightened, angry.

Wine couldn't hold the cease-fire.
An empty table, napkins on the floor
cold wind pushing against a closing door.

This Saturday Afternoon

While Parkening plays Rodrigo, I hear
Miles Davis' Reflections in Spain
and remember a place thirty-five years ago,

a wood fire, wine and candles, bull fight
pictures on the wall, red and black pillows,
and throw rugs on a hardwood floor.

She was a violinist, loved Davis and Mozart.
Her short black hair, cut exact, her skin smooth.
Her brown eyes laughed with me, then looked away.

On this Saturday afternoon
I can't remember her name.

Questions

My first weekend , first time in bed
with this beautiful young woman

>	I said, "Why don't we get married?"
>	She said, "Yes."

I didn't have the courage to back out,
a long time ago.

Recently,

>	I asked, "How was it,
>		being married to me nineteen years?"

>	She said, "Mostly unbearable.
>		If you had not left, I would have left you."

>	She said, "It took me fifteen years
>		to recover from the damage."

Then to our son,

>	I asked, "How it was for you
>		having me for a father?"

>	He said, "It fell short."

Alone

You lay beside her
      sleepless, jaw clenched,
turned over and over,
      a mile between you.

You couldn't reach out —
      touch her.
If only you could have said two words,
      "Hold me."

How It Is

When I stand close
To a Matisse painting,
Colored flat shapes,

When I back off
Images come alive,
Flowers, dancers.

When I stand close
You shrink and become
Flat like a mirror.

When I look back
At your color picture
And poster smile

I feel a deep, long,
Covered-over trench
Behind your door.

When I stand back
From a Matisse painting
I am embraced.

A Gift Remembered

Tonight a string quartet plays and my mind
flashes way back – 1939.

It was late and I had two beers and a bag of chips.
That same quartet in F by Ravel was playing.

Chamber music became a compass,
a guide for me through storms I created in my life.

Sonatas, trios, quartets, Bach,
Vivaldi, Haydn, Ravel, Prokofiev.

So many nights their music
nursed me back into the world.

How many ever in a lifetime discover
anymore than survival?

Home At Last

I've had mail delivered to forty places,
twenty before I got married, thirteen
with four wives, seven alone.

I traveled endless miles on the ground,
half a million in the air, didn't sleep well
in hundreds of motels and hotels.

Eighteen years ago with my last wife, we built
our last home, a mile off a country road
on a ridge surrounded by mountains.

Until five years ago my old dog
waited stretched out in the driveway
when I drove to town.

When I returned she raised her head,
wagged her tail once, struggled to stand,
welcomed me home.

For the First Time

I am alone on New Year's eve
in our round pine house
high on a Siskiyou ridge.

It took seven years
to build this place overlooking
a small river valley.

Light snow is falling. A hot cast iron
wood stove pushes the cold away.
Ashkenazy is playing Mozart.

Wolfgang remembered me in his will.
My hands dance and I follow
in a circle of small steps.

The Prize

My house rides a ridge circled
by fir and pine. South, a little Matterhorn,
snow-covered half the year.

I walk mountain trails. Coyote, deer,
rattle snake, and skunk are neighbors,
black bear and cougar rare visitors.

I live alone, an apprentice poet
excited, astonished to be alive,
that my body waited for me to wake.
I cook for myself, as for a lover.

My old dog waits for a walk and a barn cat
flirts to be held, massaged, and drools
on my lap. If no mackerel at meal time
she looks, turns, and walks away.

First Snow Today

A mountain dirt road, Doug fir,
ponderosa pine and madrone
reach and vibrate in cold wet wind.

Pot-holes, ponds and ditches
are covered with brown leaves
from white oaks.

A man moves dry firewood into his house.
His old dog doesn't eat,
whimpers and falls.

He decides to put her away
next Wednesday if
she lasts that long.

Here and Now

I don't hear a knock on my door, see
a flashing light, or feel a breeze
suggesting a path to a shore.

I count strokes and cross my river.
The only one watching is me, arms
reaching are mine. A shadow somewhere,
waits for the end of my story.

Any day is the right day, every day a miracle
to be grateful for, to wonder about,
to reach for possibilities.

An oboe, a Douglas fir, it's spring,
wind and rain wash new leaves,
buds break out on a cherry tree.

It's almost more than I can bear.

Always Questions

An honored citizen, I don't have
to make money or promises.
Some say I talk louder,
philosophize without invitation.

I am skilled at that. Demons
no longer hold me hostage.
Fear has no hard grip, pain
mostly about attitude.

Maybe something is missing.
Is it rapture, wild inspiration?
A friend suggests spirituality.
He means God. I nod and walk away.

OM NAMAH SHIVAYA
Thank you, spirit within me

Some nights curiosity keeps me awake.

Saga

You crossed an ocean in a kayak
in winter and woke on a beach
above high tide grateful to be alive.

Seagulls settle, face the sea,
sandpipers chase the surf,
stab bubbles in wet sand.

On the horizon a ship disappears
carrying a lifetime of duties, games
faces and toys. You have everything
you need, want, not a collector anymore.

Entropy your partner and you dance
in ever expanding circles. Somewhere
a door into darkness.

An Invitation

I circled a gazebo of Tibetan prayer wheels,
each passage a year remembered, lost moments,

>   where I leaped before I looked,
>   left the barn door open,
>   didn't make a stitch in time,
>   printed before I edited.

I might cancel insurance,
>   sell possessions,
>   invest everything in the moment,

step, eyes open, through a blind door.

Old Photographs

of babies growing up, those
who grew old. Lightness in some
and the tired ones, so many gone.

My great grandmother, born 1839
stern, head cocked, eyes clear.

My father and my son in uniform each
twenty-two years old seventy-seven years apart,
like brothers at attention.

My picture is in the mirror, an old man
looks at me with soft wet eyes.

The Finish Line

For years on the twelve-mile drive
to town past alfalfa fields, pear orchards,
need-paint barns and farm houses

I often passed an old couple walking briskly
always holding hands. They waved, I honked,
always looked forward to their golden smiles.

For months they were gone. Just
a country road, duck ponds, horses in pastures,
bent mail boxes, old crooked fences.

One day the man, alone,
walking slower waved without looking,
without smiling, just there.

Age Like a Desert

knocks on my door. I camp high
in a nest of gray boulders. Summer
long and dry, the Mojave sparse –
chilled desolation. A gray sky
pretending the possibility of rain.

In a dry wash, on a seemingly dead bush,
I find a corolla of radiant violet petals,
circling a gold crown. I kneel, tremble,
hands on my knees—lean close, and ask,

    "How can you exist in this place?"
A voice in my head answers,
    "Old plants can have beautiful flowers."

Awake this whole night, my eyes on stars.
Was that violet flower part of a dream?
At dawn, I move in expanding circles
and there it is.

Without thinking I pour water from
my canteen on the parched sand.
Again the voice, irritated,
    "Appreciate me, don't help me."

Back and Forth

Remember long ago when we
couldn't grow older quick enough,
wanted to be ten at six, sixteen at ten,
twenty-one at sixteen, at least for boys.

This reaching to be older went on
for a long time till about forty-five.
Fifty gave birth to denial, so fifty
was like forty, women thirty smiled.

Sixty was like fifty but seventy
was seventy, and each year from then on
was old and older. Nothing to do
with how I felt. At seventy-five, hold on.

In the Ophthamologist's office I was one
of a bunch of old patients holding on
to sight. In the Orthopedic's office, again
holding on, I was with those wanting to walk a ways.

The trick is to stay active, invest in health,
be generous, ever curious, walk strong
but don't misjudge the intent of
a younger woman's smile.

What About It

Ever try telling people under seventy,
how it feels to be old? Their usual reply –

> "Never say you are old. You are
> only as old as you feel."

I had an idea about getting old when I became
less sure footed, needed replacement parts,
felt different in the younger world, sometimes
    invisible.

We move away from each other; the young
trapped in the judgments of the old,
the old, constant reminders of the inevitable.

The young, doing reruns of the older's
mistakes. For the old, regrets better forgotten.
If I had not married that woman. Wait!
What about our children and their children?

Observation

These days dry skin on my arms
resembles lake waves with white caps
heading for shore.

With pressure toward my wrist
ridges form like rows of cord
wrapped around a bat handle.

When I point my arm upward,
with fingers spread, the skin on
the back of my hand cascades down

like fine silk over raised
tendons, bones and veins like
Michelangelo's sculpture.

More Than Meets the Eye

A chair, a table, a window,
almost enough for a still life.
The table for meals, conversation,
sorting junk mail, paying bills.

The other day I looked,
I mean I looked through the window
and there, near, an apple tree
blooming,

then an oak with new leaves.
Beyond was the ponderosa pine
I planted eighteen years ago
now grown thirty feet tall.

I am an inch shorter.

Lightness of Being

A faint ding-ding alarm
tilts an unfinished dream,
triggers morning ritual.

After water unlocks my dry mouth
relief commands first place,
takes the longest time.

A "WANTED" photo in the mirror,
thin white hair in disarray,
droop lids over squinty eyes,
night creases in a day face.

A shower and shave bring
hundreds of facial muscles
to attention, build a daytime smile.

My right foot enters my shorts easily
the left, another mystery.

Spring Cleaning

I am impatient with people who ask,
        "Why am I here?"
           "What am I supposed to do?"
    and look for answers
    from somewhere.

Those questions never mattered.
        To be seduced
    by towering mountains
    and raging seas,
        there's something!

I have no time now for people
        who live inside circled wagons
    buried in possessions
    and bottom fish
        with old war stories.

Old Soldier

Captain Richard was slow to rise,
would not stand for long, his spirit failing.
He became picky if everything wasn't simple.

Anais Nin and Evergreen stories became a bore.
One night the Captain retired. Together for a lifetime,
without the Captain . . . who would I be?

All the tours of duty we shared, strategic planning
at night in camp. Sometimes anticipation
of the campaign was better than the field action,

less trouble, no fear of defeat.
When I accepted the Captain's decision
I felt lighter, an obligation released.

No more duty to perform, expectations to live up to.
Some nights I remember the good times
and we hold each other and dance

perhaps to march again in the right parade.

I Want to Talk

to you my son about the deep space
between us. I want to tell you I know
our family was never a source of joy,
never a warm safe house. I want to tell you

I didn't know myself, or your mother. She was
beautiful, accepted an offer I didn't mean, didn't
take back. We soon knew being together
was a mistake we survived for nineteen years.

Your mother and I each grew up
in cold houses, ran away, never
willing to reach out with open hearts.
With your sister we were a family

wanting to keep warm in an endless winter.
Each of us found ways to deal with loneliness.
As a boy I found duty and obligation a means
of exchange that seduced and confused,

allowed me judgment and resentment.
I split and built two shorter failed families
and then the last one, the best, lasted
twenty years. I am alone, grateful

to be alive, and sad. So here we are,
you, fifty and me seventy-eight, stuck.
It can get better.

I want to talk.

What Then?

A stub, once young and whole,
lies in a VA hospital basket,
a no-name remnant from a war.

Dalton Trumbo called one Johnny
in a novel, just a body with a stubborn heart
and a short life to remember.

After many soft touches
he would nod his head.
How many senses could I lose

and still be grateful for a life of only
memories and dreams? What if I
got bored, couldn't tell anyone

and couldn't turn it off? An old being
with clouded eyes, out of touch,
tired of waiting?

Summer Writers In Iowa City

From the prison-like dormitory,
a road, a path, and a river lie
side by side, North and South,
fifty cars a minute on the road.

A slow walker on the path,
a stick floats on the river
moves a mile in an hour.
The walker covers two miles.

The cars roar, click over grooves.
The walker watches ducks,
people on grass, shadows,
drivers with blank faces.

Writers are here, excited,
ignored by locals and students
in a kingdom of bureaucrats
and tenured professors.

ODE TO A PROFESSOR

Aspiring attendees listen
to his every word, pray for recognition,
affirmation, attention. He is

tenured at the prime facility for MFA poets.
His stories about his peers and sports
in Chicago fill a morning.

Might he be tired, after thirty-five years
writing and teaching, over and over? After
he reveals the secret of poetry,

        read and write,

he listens to fourteen eager poets,
each waiting for a turn at bat,
hoping for a home run.

ALLIHIES
Beare Peninsula, County Cork, Ireland

A sloping plain rises from the Atlantic,
land unevenly divided by rock walls,
a mosaic of fields of greens and golds.

Stone houses crouch like sentries posted
around a curved village of clustered buildings
with four pubs, a church, and two graveyards.

Harringtons, Kellys, Murphys, O'Shaughnessys,
O'Sheas and more farm and fish, hard lives.
Outsiders remain blow–ins a long time.

Atlantic storms hold everything hostage,
everyone on watch; the Church, shelter
for the soul, the pubs, banks of available joy.

Irish spirit, tempered by centuries
of resistance and survival, endures,
keeps song, stories, and place alive.

New Mexico Story

On a Sangre De Cristo mountain
north of Taos, purple lupin
clings to an alpine ledge.

Far below an endless sea,
great cones and ridges
in shades of brown and gray,

silent story tellers
of floods of ice, claws of wind,
and a deep river-cut gorge.

Late afternoon sun moves
down the sky, gray mist
dusts the sea below. Darkness

chases a sky of dying orange coals.
A curtain falls on a jagged horizon
and slowly turns to ashes.

Progress Report

Rain cascades through maple trees,
splashes on mud smeared leaves, yellows,
deep reds on root-tilted sidewalks
to rhythms of clicking studded tires.

Leaves crowd in gutter pools like
the city that buries farms and small towns
under factories, office buildings,
ding-batt housing, and strip malls.

New people arrive, fill jobs, find friends,
rent apartments, attach to winning teams,
satisfy wild desires and basic needs
with plastic and 19 percent fees.

And Trees and Beetles Know

Square-saw a downed, dead Doug fir,
97 tight annual rings in a small trunk,
a story of slow rain on a tough south slope
after a seven year drought.

Out of beetles always present,
larvae circle the trunk, like a tight noose,
cut drought-thick sap veins, kill the tree.

Needles brown and branches break,
dead sentries stand in the forest.
Beetles move on like a wolf-pack in an elk herd.
Dry roots loosen like an old man's teeth.

Wind teeters a corpse off-center.
One day or night on a slow-start arc
it gathers momentum, crashes,
bounces, and crunches apart.

Small trees long in shadow wait
to bathe in sunlight, thirsty to inherit
scarce moisture when rains return.

It's Not That Far From Here

Slivers of moonlight dance on eucalyptus leaves.
A path leads to a highway along cliffs
and the east end of the Pacific Ocean.

Head south, balance on the white line,
a tightrope on a road moving into shadow.
No cars, surf crashing rocks twenty stories below.

Out of shadow, under a full moon, on your left
an arm's length away, a dark figure walks
in silence, in step, you wonder, face straight.

Suddenly he is gone. You climb the roadside
boulder barrier, sit, legs over the side
high above the smashing surf. Your hands

behind you unsure, to hold or push. A cloud
moves under the moon, pours darkness
into the void below. You rock back and forth

playing chicken.

Now Showing

In the movies a guy can get stomped,
smashed in the face, kicked in the balls,
and in the next scene he has a clean
shaven face, not even a limp.

Off camera an army of first-aid
doctors and nurses must move in,
tape ribs, sew up cut lips and eyebrows,
install trusses to send the star back

into the next scene to rescue
and seduce the leading lady
while typhoons and terrorists
blow buildings apart.

Oh! The ear-splitting sounds
of destruction, the blood and guts,
the audience full of popcorn, miles
from bills, work, and consciousness.

Reincarnation

A tall ponderosa pine high
on an eastern slope of a Siskiyou mountain,

a cone on a branch, seeds in the cone
blown loose to float and land on soft moist earth.

A cradle warmed by sunlight nursed by rain drops
while time watches a new forest being born.

Not the First Time

An afternoon lightning strike, in no time
an inferno. Trees explode into poles of fire
thirty stories high, creatures zig-zag, crazy.

Firefighters drop trees, smother hot spots. Dozers
carve fire breaks, tankers dump retardant. Wind
reverses on the sixth day. A choked fire surrenders.

A week later at noon, the orange sun, quarter size,
squints through brown smoke at blackened slopes
covered with gray-white ash as in a nuclear winter.

Mirror

Mindless silent watcher of passage ways,
bedroom frolics and battles. Never
a give-away like Nixon's tapes.

Peeping Tom always waiting,
never caring. Imagine the stories,
jokes, crimes to be told.

Watcher of children
hooked on television, a box
too small for their brains.

An invisible house sitter,
a watch dog no one hears,
film-less camera that never tells lies.

Last Day 1995

Saw-tooth black fir trees
        silhouettes
               on a steel-gray curtain
        reaching blue lakes
              in white clouds
        a patchwork-quilt sky

On this last day
        shirt-sleeve warm.

Behind Copland's "Rodeo"
        a tiny quartz clock
              ticks last seconds
                     endings
          beginnings

Will I choose differently next year?
        to clean up place   space
          for coming tomorrows
      new mysteries
           possibilities

By midnight   quiet sleep.

On Christmas Morning

A wet hawk perched on the top
of a forty foot ponderosa pine
just outside my window. Like
a British high magistrate turning

slowly in flashing silence from
east to west to east, from time to time
shaking away a spray of rain drops.
His head of fine curled almost white feathers

like a judge's wig cascading over wings pulled
in like shoulders under a great dark cloak.
A beacon, a radar antenna turning slowly
watching and being seen.

A Day on Twenty-Third Street

Sun whisks roof tops and dormers
on a cool August morning. Coffee
machines primed for early birds. Trucks
eat yesterday's garbage, exhaust
thickens, joggers flash by.
You stop for the morning paper.

A young man hesitates,
"Some coins, Sir, I'm hungry."
       "What do you do?"
"I ask people for money, I'm hooked on alcohol,
got no cigarettes, gotta get some food."

He is thin, small, and tense,
dark patches under bloodshot eyes,
isn't dirty. A foam pad strapped
on his back, a soiled Dodgers cap
visor forward. He makes eye contact.

You give him three quarters and ask.
       "What's the game plan?"
"I don't have one, just day by day –
the wine bottle owns me."
       "Sounds like a one-sided deal!"
His eyes go soft and wet.
       "And a tough one."

You turn, touch his shoulder –
his right hand presses your arm
and you walk on.

II

By afternoon it turns hot, corner
telephone poles plastered with distractions,
Calamity Jam, Radio Fires, Chatty Hattie
Hungry Mob, Boogie Shoes, and lots more.

Rows of old buildings stare at each other
                          across a narrow two-lane street.
Eateries, cheap and dear, grape leaves,
pasta, burgers, sushi, burritos –
beer joints, and bakeries.

Shops offer pretty-penny attachments
for precious bodies, walls, and space.
Parking limited to thirty minutes.
Kids buzz and swarm, tourists wander –
munch pizza, pluck cheese strands,
suck large sugar drinks. Thin women
walk straight and fast, right on target.

On a hospital street corner, a teenage crowd
listens to a young woman screaming,
        "Yes! Animal rights! Are we going to fight?"
The crowd shouts, over and over.
        "Yes! Yes!"
Posters, handbills, the hospital kills cats.

You want to play judge and say,
        "Scream loud. Flail. Don't stop and wonder."
and then you remember, being alone
with nothing else to do, easy to be seduced
by games with strangers.
You back off – and turn away.

III

Teenagers on the make under the quarter moon
smoke, conspire, some with skin pierced,
threaded, and tattooed in tight jeans,
tank tops, short skirts. Hungry faces
with dying eyes scan for single male drivers.

Crowded cafes fill with restless souls
men and women, men paired, women paired
in chic threads, grunge and rings—
blossoms in the city night.

By midnight the crowd gone, street empty.
Shadow men push shopping carts for treasure.
A copy shop and hospital open all night.

You have been invisible the whole day, except
for a panhandler, and your reflection
in a dark shop window.

No Change For The Bus

The bus shelter leans
into hard Santa Fe wind.
A young woman sits inside
moves two shopping bags to make room.

I sit and ask if she has change.
She laughs and hands me two-bits,
says in a barrio lilt,
"Hey man, no problem, pass it on."

Loose curls, thick lashes, lined eyes,
all black on smooth white skin, straight
teeth, her red-red lips ask
"What's your trip?"
        "A poetry workshop."
"Recite a poem for me."
        "I don't memorize."

She laughs, worn hands push hair away,
fingers covered with costume rings.

        "You ever write?" I ask.
"I read some books."
        "What kind?"
"Action, drama, passion. Hate detail."

I watch her swing-walk onto the bus,
tight black pants, loose white jacket.
The driver and two passengers call her name.
She laughs and snaps her fingers.

We Just Keep Rolling Along

A yellow bus prowls back roads,
stops traffic with flashing red lights,
scoops up unsuspecting recruits
to be taught the myth that there is —
a there there.

Yellow bus windows with little heads,
like "Peanuts" bobbing up and down.
Of forty kids on that bus ten
will drop out. Four may finish college.
One may become a teacher.

In twenty-five years many will be
single parents, few will read books.
Several will attend addiction programs.
Some will abuse spouses and children.
Many will not bother to vote.

And the good news!

The ones with kids
will put them on a yellow bus.
Out of every one-hundred buses
there might escape—-one poet.

Oasis

He sailed through South Dakota slouched
on his red Indian bike, ponytail flying,
weathered tattooed arms through leather,
black gloved hands loose on the bars.

He slowed down in the next town, nine hundred
and fifty seven souls, tree-lined streets, buildings
from the twenties, peaceful, not too many flags.
He'd give it a shot, find a burger and a beer.

In a shaded park he settled against an oak
older than the town, wolfed the burger down,
rolled a joint, took a long drag, and dozed
till a thump on his boot.

He opened to shined black boots up past
a hanging belly, fat face, tight mustache,
dark glasses, to a red nose that smelled
hippie and dope.

Windows watched him trudge
in a slow-motion parade and then bow
and walk through the jail door.

His dinner tray arrived as he watched
a spider eat a fly. Under the napkin
there was a yellow daisy.

Long Red Manicured Nails

She slightly drags her feet, walks slow,
head clutched by a small brim hat, her coat
faded tan hangs, old slippers cover white socks.

Frayed white gloves grasp a red purse strap.
Her lined face sags into a sunken chest. Her eyes tearful,
two front teeth missing, her smile pleads.

She enters the diner almost every morning,
for a bowl of oatmeal and buttered toast
and afternoons for a half-sandwich and cup of soup.

Each time she takes off her gloves, eats slowly,
reads newspapers. Her clean fingers
have perfectly manicured long red nails.

On the first day of each month she comes early,
waits quietly, asks, "How much
do I owe you for the month, please?"

The owner says, "Three dollars."

Memories of Emma Lou

I found you again at seventy-five,
a tenured professor, riding your bicycle.
I was impressed by your papers
on digs and studies of early man.

Still a political activist and member
of the sexual liberation league, I loved
your wild humor when you showed
me your backyard marijuana crop.

After your stroke at eighty-two you
didn't need your pick, old boots, torn Levis,
You ate with your left hand, head cocked,
same blue eyes, quick mind, crooked smile.

I held you, massaged your twisted body.
Tears in our eyes when I read you Rilke.
You were eighty-four when you died.

Richard Feynman

"I want to know what it feels like
to be an electron."

He liked to play. Everything
was something new, no history.

He picked locks at Los Alamos,
solved equations in a topless bar,

won the Nobel Prize in physics
for work he did when he was twenty-three.

He found the cause of the Challenger disaster
with a rubber band and a glass of ice water.

His last words, "This dying is boring."

Later his friend dreamed they were talking.
"Hey Richard, how come you're talking, you're dead?"
"Oh well, at least we won't get interrupted this way."

I. Goodbye, Tony

An Irish priest from Africa,
a fast friendship, we played like boys
at camp. It hurt when he left.

A long time later I wrote. My letter
returned, an unsigned note attached.

> "We are very sorry to tell you, Father Tony Dalton
> passed away in 1984. He is now with his God."

Recently, a chance meeting
with another priest from Africa,
I asked about Father Dalton.

> "Tony died while hang gliding."

II. Invitation

To dive off a cliff
on a hang glider,
ride risk with eagles.

To taste life and be afraid.
To let full breaths tingle.
      A way to play.

Maybe getting hurt
is no big deal, you heal, or
welcome to another way.

Jack's Story

Joe died and I stepped up,
my father pointed the way.

Harvard and weather vanes,
my family everywhere.

I carried the ball tight,
winning was what was done.

It was November, 1962
I needed to go south,

to ride in the open air
for duty, sun and cloudless sky.

Enlightenment Next Stop

The third day orange-clad Poona
devotees from the world over trembled
on a first-class passage to Samadhi.

When HE enters the hall,
orgasms like corn popping,
the universe at attention.

When HIS hands move
all bodies like swan necks follow
in unison, eyes streaming.

HE, the soul-guide to freedom
from the wheel of desire and suffering.
Drums beat louder, faster.

Everyone wild, moving like lightning, then
a raging orange sea crashes in silence.
The moment is a step closer.

Midnight IT would happen
or someday, they say.

Winner Takes All

He travels, lives anywhere
in high style, pays for,
gets anything he desires,
doesn't trust liberals,

survived by-pass surgery,
treasures gourmet food,
controls his kids with trust funds,
his wife closed down, preserved.

He often lies awake, hostage
of random thoughts, lost
in wild dreams where every door
he knocks on is opened

by a stranger or no one.

Event

An angel opens her heart, impales
herself on the Washington Monument
searching for Lincoln's smile.

Spider webs lash out
screaming, "Water the river!"
Senators run for cover.

Flocks of garlic dance in moonlight
writing sonnets to Robert Bly.
Fighter pilots pour soy milk over Tulsa.

Rednecks elect Jane Fonda president.
Clinton and Yeltsin resign, become nuns,
Arabs and Jews make love.

Corn-ball poets get the Nobel Prize
Creation shudders, the world stumbles,
wobbles, circles on and on.

Look Away

Street children beg,
find food in garbage cans,
sell their bodies.

Anything to survive,
to find a place to sleep,
perhaps to dream.

A story often started
in the belly of an unprotected girl
or a woman too tired to care.

Some of us have tunnel vision,
hold every conception sacred,
new human life at any price.

Then we look away
               look away
                            look away
                                         look away.

One Camera Angle

of a system that chooses dividends over jobs,
drives the stock market up as employees
are thinned out like weak animals from a herd.

A market driven economy classifies wage earners
an expendable commodity. Unemployment keeps
unhealthy people competing for low wage work.

Politicians and pundits wave sheets of paper, promote
family values, blame immigrants, environmentalists,
high taxes, people on welfare and sinners.

Welfare saps will, keeps hungry people tame, victims
of survival fatigue, confused, indifferent, listening
without discrimination to voices that tap their fears.

So few are looking at weather vanes and barometers
and self interest is a scab covering greedy eyes.

What Is It Going to Be?

Many men cling to past power,
horizons fade away, the present
slowly loses focus, walls close in,
and doors no longer used, lock.

Flowers are not watered, film covers tired eyes.

A giant oak, lightning-split,
the largest part on the ground,
rotting, covered with moss, home
for scurrying creatures.

On top of the standing trunk,
a crooked limb, green leaves
reaching, battle flag flying
for a downed giant.

Year End

Christmas carols flip a switch, darkness
encloses you. Your wheels spin and you
drop into a steep walled well of sadness.
Memories dissolve bindings holding tears.

What is happening?

A voice, your own, whispers, "Wait, just wait.
Don't open a bottle. Don't smoke
a joint, Don't make any phone calls.
Don't shut down, stay awake. Just listen.

Now, you are alone.

Now, you are old dealing with worn joints.
It has never been joyous at year's end
and you are in a place you never
allowed before.

You can't run. You can't hide."

Your voice calls your name. You listen,
you soften, and you listen.

Biography

Clair Killen was born in Canada in 1920. He lived most of his life in southern California. The mountains of southern Oregon have been his home for the last twenty years. He began to write after attending the summer 1993 Writer's Workshop at Southern Oregon State College with Lawson Inada.

Jacksonville, Oregon

COLOPHON

The type for the text is Berthold Baskerville 10 on 13pt., named after the legendary printer/publisher John Baskerville (1706-1775). Adapted by Bruce Rogers in 1917 and collected for the Monotype Corporation in 1924, the Berthold typefoundry in Germany created this variance now leased to Adobe. Offset printed with soy inks and recycled paper by Kate Hitt at the Many Names Press printshop in Soquel, California. Edition limited to 500 copies.